TAOISM:

THE MAGIC, THE MYSTICISM

Julius Evola

Translated, with an Introduction,
by Guido Stucco
St. Louis University,
Department of Theology

Foreword by Jean Bernachot

ORIENTAL
CLASSICS

—HOLMES—

ISBN # 1-55818-227-6

THIRD EDITION,

REVISED

— 2006 —

I wish to dedicate this translation
to Susan Pitol
Maiores Pennas Nido

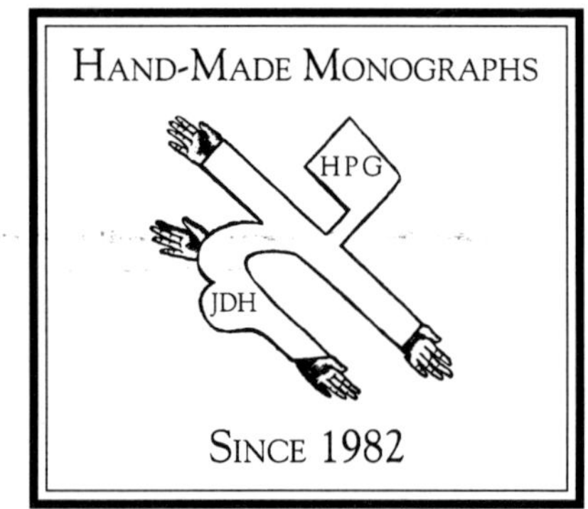

ORIENTAL CLASSICS
HOLMES PUBLISHING GROUP LLC
POSTAL BOX 2370
SEQUIM WA 98382 USA
JDHOLMES.COM

INTRODUCTION

Who was Julius Evola? Considered by many a philosopher, others have cast him in the role of arch-reactionary. Regardless, his philosophical writings have earned him a place as one of the leading representatives of the Traditionalist school.

Like the American poet Ezra Pound before him, the term "fascist" has been accorded Evola for being among the opposition during WWII. For three decades he was shunned by the academic community which took little interest in his writings. Yet Evola has been the object of an interesting revival, acquiring a posthumous revenge of sorts. Conferences and *symposia* devoted to the analysis of his thought have "mushroomed" in the past fifteen years throughout Europe. Secondly, Evola has exercised a magical spell on many people who, having lost faith in so-called progressive ideals, have taken a sharp turn toward Tradition in a quest for something "more transcendent" or for something of a "higher order." These new views cannot be readily found in the wasteland of contemporary society. Thirdly, his spiritual and metaphysical ideas, far from being an appendix to his *Weltanschauung*, represent the very core and can no longer be ignored. Evola's ideas call for a critical analysis and a reasonable response from sympathizers and critics alike.

The reader of these monographs will be able to find detailed information about Julius Evola's life and thought in Richard Drake's writings.[1] This introduction seeks to identify and to characterize the common themes running through all of the following treatises:—*The Path of Enlightenment in the Mithraic Mysteries*; *Zen: The Religion of the Samurai*; *Taoism, The Magic, The Mysticism*; *Rene Guenon: A Teacher for Modern Times*. (Holmes Publishing Group, 1994.) Let us begin with the first theme.

Upon a cursory reading, it is immediately evident that Evola establishes a dichotomy between common, ordinary knowledge, and a secret knowledge which is the prerogative of a selected few. This distinction, also known to Plato, who distinguished between *doxa* and *episteme*, has been the legacy of the Mystery cults, of Mithraism, of Gnosticism, and of all initiatory chains, East or West.

The epistemological distinction between esoteric and exoteric knowledge is rooted, according to Evola, in the ontological classism which separates people, the multitudes, or the *oi polloi*, from the *aristoi*, the heroes, the kings, and the men of knowledge (priests and ascetics). One of the constants in Evola's thought, is his aversion for the empirical subject, who lives, eats, reproduces and dies; everything in his works represents a yearning for something which is more than ordinary existence, more than that condition of life which is heavily conditioned by routines, passions, cravings and superficiality, for what the Germans call *meher als leben* ("more than living"),—a sort of nostalgia for the *Hyperuranium*, for Transcendence, for "what was in the origins." Esotericism is the means to achieve the ultimate reality which all religions strive to achieve, though they call it by many names, as the late Joseph Campbell was fond of saying. During his career as a writer, Julius Evola was involved in an extensive, sophisticated study of esoteric doctrines. In these monographs we find Evola celebrating the metaphysical premises and techniques of Zen and of operative Taoism; elsewhere he sang the praise of Tantrism[2] and of early Buddhism.[3] In another work, commended by Carl G. Jung, he discussed Hermeticism.[4] Scholars of various disciplines will not forgive this controversial and brilliant Italian thinker his incursions in their own fields of competence, such as history, religion, mythology, and psychology. And yet Evola succeeds in weaving a colorful and suggestive pattern, which slowly and gracefully evolves into a well articulated, monolithic *Weltanschauung*.

Another distinctive feature of these works is Julius Evola's firm conviction in the existence of a hierarchy to which all states of being are subject. These states defy the imagination of ordinary people. In the Western religious tradition one does not easily find an articulated cosmology or for that matter a serious emphasis on the soul's experiences in its quest for God. There are the powerful exceptions represented by the writings of St. Bonaventure, St. John of the Cross, Jacob Boehme, St. Theresa of Avila, and other more obscure mystics. Since the personal God of theism is believed to have brought the universe into being, Christianity's focus, in terms of cult and speculation, has shifted from the *cosmos* to its Creator. Evola's knowledge of the Christian tradition was not equal to the erudition he displayed in other subjects. Nevertheless, he attempted to fill what he considered a vacuum in the Christian system. In the monograph dedicated to Mithras he describes the states of being or the spiritual experiences of the initiate to Mithraic mystery tradition and wisdom. These Mithraic experiences are depicted as three-dimensional, heroic, cosmological and esoteric and are juxtaposed to the two-dimensional, devotional, liturgical and exoteric spiritual experiences of formal Christianity. In the work on Zen he celebrates the hierarchical "five grades of merit," through which the initiate grows in wisdom and pursues the personal quest for enlightenment.

A third and final characteristic found in these selections is the rejection of theism and the polemics with Christianity, which in the piece on Guenon is merely outlined, but see his comparison of the Christian and the initiatory views of immortality, found in this work on Taoism. His penetrating critique of theism was articulated in the name of "higher" principles and not by an *a priori* hostility to religion and to the concepts of supernatural authority and revelation. What he rejected in theism was the idea of faith, of devotion, of abandonment in a higher power. To faith, he opposed experience; to devotion, heroic and ascetical action; to the God of theism, who is believed to be the ultimate reality, as well as the believer's goal and eschatological hope, Evola opposed the ideal of liberation and of enlightenment as you will find in the examination of Mithraism.

These monographs are a testimony to the restless curiosity and spiritual hunger of a nonspecialist who dared to venture into the domain of scholars and of specialized disciplines, only to extract precious gems of wisdom, unburdened by technical details and *minutiae* which are the obsession of scholars and of university professors. It is my sincere hope that interest in Julius Evola and his ideas will be generated by the translation of these monographs as they represent only a small portion of many untranslated works which have yet to be brought to the attention of the English speaking world.

NOTES

[1] Richard Drake, "Julius Evola and the Ideological Origins of the Radical Right in Contemporary Italy," in *Political Violence and Terror: Motifs and Motivations*, ed., Peter Merkl (Berkeley: University of California Press, 1986), 61-89; "Julius Evola, Radical Fascism and the Lateran Accords," *The Catholic Historical Review* 74 (1988): 403-19; and "The Children of the Sun," chapter in *The Revolutionary Mystique and Terrorism in Contemporary Italy* (Bloomington: Indiana University Press, 1989).

[2] Julius Evola, *The Yoga of Power*, trans. Guido Stucco (Rochester, VT: Inner Traditions, 1992).

[3] Julius Evola, *The Doctrine of the Awakening*, trans. G. Mutton (London: Luzac Co, 1951).

[4] Julius Evola, *The Hermetic Tradition*, trans. E. Rhemus (Rochester, VT: Inner Traditions, 1993).

FOREWORD

The following text, which Evola wrote in 1959, was the introduction to an Italian translation of the *Tao-Te-Ching*. This differs from a similar piece he wrote in 1923, which reflected the trajectories characteristic of his "philosophical period."

In his *Rivolta contro il mondo moderno* [Revolt Against the Modern World], which was written as an analysis of the rise and fall of civilizations, Evola quotes the following passage from the *Tao-Te-Ching*.

When the Tao was lost, its attributes appeared; when its attributes were lost, benevolence appeared; when benevolence was lost, righteousness appeared; and when righteousness was lost, the proprieties appeared. Now propriety is the attenuated form of whole-heartedness and good faith, and is also the commencement of disorder.[1]

Since Western civilization has already reached the lowest stage of its decadence, it would be interesting to seek to identify the potential for a partial restoration, by moving through the various phases of involution, one step at a time, but on an upward pathway. In this essay, Evola is not asking his readers to commit themselves to such a task. On the contrary, he pursues the elements necessary to acquire personal realization. These elements are to be found in a now remote tradition, both spatially and temporally. Paradoxically, the teachings of very distant civilizations are more alive in the cities of the Western world than the "wisdom" of Western civilization.

In the following, Evola explains the quest for a direct relationship with the supernatural dimension and its origin, but without the "mediation" of any religion. Evola's considerations on Taoism, written on the *tabula rasa* of Western civilization, are formulated in rigorous fashion. These conclusions are straight-to-the-point and void of sentimentalism and may represent, next to other paths such as early Buddhism or Zen, an introduction to a method of reintegrating one's true "self" and true "center." At least this will be pertinent for the specific human type who still possesses, though in a latent state, the sense of transcendence.

Jean Bernachot

TAOISM

According to tradition, Lao-tzu and Confucius were contemporaries. The former lived between 570 and 490 B.C.; the latter between 552 and 479 B.C. Their teachings do not represent something new but rather are a reformulation and adaptation of the primordial Eastern tradition based on the *I-Ching* and its commentaries. This reformulation became necessary due to a partial dulling and dimming of that tradition. Both Lao-tzu and Confucius participated in this reformulation, though from two different perspectives. Because of the difference between these two perspectives, people often claimed to notice an antithesis (which in truth is only relative) between the Taoist and the Confucian teachings. Lao-tzu's doctrine essentially has a metaphysical and initiatory nature, even in its ethical and social ramifications, while Confucius' doctrine is centered on the moral, social and political dimensions. The Taoist ideal is the disciple who is and who acts beyond all possible limitations, beginning with the limitations rooted in himself. The Confucian ideal, conversely, is limited to an ideal typical of human culture, namely to the ideal of the "noble man," who, in the context of political society, develops a style and an uprightness through the practice of some positive virtues and through specific behavioral patterns.

While Confucius prefers a rational approach, Lao-tzu employs paradox as an hermeneutical tool. Lao-tzu develops non-conformist views and professes a subtle wisdom, which is often expressed in mysterious, elusive and bewildering terms. These two approaches are contradictory only when either one is perceived as absolute and final. Only a particular version of Confucianism, which degenerated into the Mandarins' formalism and into a system of external precepts, is antithetical to the essentially metaphysical doctrine of Lao-tzu. According to the Chinese historian Ssa Ma Chien, Confucius uttered this statement after meeting Lao-tzu: "It is possible to set a trap in order to catch animals; it is possible to catch fishes with nets and to catch birds with arrows. But how will one capture the dragon which flies in the air, above the clouds? Today I have seen Lao-tzu. He reminded me of the dragon."

On the other hand, in Taoist writings, beginning with Lieh-tzu's, Confucius is often portrayed as a disciple of Lao-tzu, or as a teacher of Taoist doctrine. All differences considered, the Chinese perceived an intimate connection between Confucian and Taoist teachings. This connection exists because both masters drew inspiration from the common source of the primordial tradition and orthodoxy.

It should be noted that Confucius' historic existence as a particular individual has been proven, and that we have rather specific details concerning his life. This is not the case with Lao-tzu; thus, one may wonder whether this name corresponded to a person or whether it was a symbolic designation. We do not even know his real name, since Lao-tzu is essentially a title. It literally means "the old child." There is a popular legend according to which he was born with the features of an old, white-bearded man. However, in Chinese tradition, old age also carries a metaphorical meaning, being a synonym of eternity and even of immortality (i.e., the correct translation of the name of a famous Chinese deity, *Hwang-Lao-Kum*, is not "Old Yellow Master," but rather "The Immortal Lord of the Center," as yellow is the color of the center).

Thus, Lao-tzu, or "Old Child," specifically designates the attributes of perennial actuality, duration and youth proper to those who maintain contact with the origins, just as the "men of Tao" are credited to have done.

According to some, Lao-tzu was a historiographer assigned to the archives of Lo, the Chou Dynasty's capital. In the ancient Chinese Empire, just as in ancient Rome, the "officials" were believed to be invested with a sacred character. Also, the "historic archives" contained the documents of tradition, and sometimes they were kept so secret that, reportedly, those in charge preferred to be put to death rather than surrender them to someone, rulers included, who could lay no claim to the privilege. Anyhow, Lao-tzu should not be considered as a bureaucrat or file clerk. Eventually, this character left his position in order to spend his life in solitude. After condensing the essence of his doctrine, he wrote a book at the invitation of the guardian of the *Han-ku* Northwestern mountain pass, and the mysterious Lao-tzu disappeared into the West and was never heard from again. He left the world of his time, and, according to the historian Sse Ma Chien, "Nobody knows where he went."

In popular legends, Lao-tzu, upon leaving the Empire, withdrew to K'un Lun, a mountain bordering Tibet. For Taoists, this mountain eventually assumed the symbolic character of a "center." There, he settled in the "Mysterious Capital," a designation which later was applied to the seat of the Yellow Turbans sect of the Taoist religion. According to other legends, Lao-tzu died at the age of 81, which is a most symbolic number, since 81 is a Taoist sacred number corresponding to Heaven and to the perfect fulfillment of the *yang* quality. It may also be noted that Lao-tzu's book consists of 81 short chapters. This fulfillment, which implies the overcoming of the transitory, generated another legend that implies Lao-tzu continued living, as one of the so-called "immortal earthlings."

According to another set of legends, either several people changed their names to "Lao-tzu," or there has been more than one person with that name. This explains the different dating ascribed to Lao-tzu by various biographers. Aside from the deification which Lao-tzu underwent in *Tao-chiao*, namely popular Taoism (just as it happened to Buddha when Buddhism turned into a religion), people fancied about a super-temporal "Lao-tzu" ("born before Heaven and Earth," reads an inscription dating toward the end of the 2nd century B.C.) who appeared under various names in thirteen consecutive existences following Fo-Hi and Cheng-Nong. This super-temporal being was an initiator of "real men" and the occult inspiration of the sacred monarchs who founded the dynasties up to and prior to the Chang and Chou Dynasties. Some even claimed that "Lao-tzu" was the founder of the T'ang dynasty. All these traditions should not be viewed as mere fictions. The positive content which can be gathered from these legends is the relationship between Lao-tzu's doctrine with a non-human influence and with an initiatory current strictly associated to the royal function.

The role of "Lao-tzu" has allegedly been played by various people, including the historic Lao-tzu, provided there ever was one. He is supposed to have continued an initiatory chain and to have been a prominent figure in it; his own name, after him, may have passed on to other members of the same chain, since in that context individual beings do not matter as such. As far as the *Tao-Te-Ching* is concerned, it certainly contains original formulations and even if there are some personal references to its author, the relationship of the doctrine found therein with the primordial tradition, has never been questioned. Aside from frequent references to the origins and to the teachers of old, during the early stages of the Han period (2nd century B.C.), it was common opinion that Taoism had begun with the first Chinese emperor, Hwang Ti (2697-2598 B.C.), the so-called "King of the Center" or "Yellow Emperor." During that time, the imperial patriarchal society displaced a matriarchal society. The sense of the ideal relationship between "Lao-tzu" and Hwang Ti was so acute, that for a long time one of the Taoist doctrines was that of *Hwang-Lao*, a term composed with parts of both names. Analogously, the *Tao-Te-Ching* was associated so closely to the *I-Ching*, that another name for the doctrine was *Lao-I*.

The works of Lieh-tzu, who was the second of the founding fathers of Taoism, were the creation of an entire trend of thought rather than the product of one individual. There is uncertainty as to whether this figure existed historically or symbolically.

We are certain, however, of the historical existence of the third founding father of Taoism, Chuang-tzu. His work abounds with personal references but the teaching expressed in it is distorted and diluted in many areas. Poetry and short stories are prevalent, in contrast to the essential, dry and shining style of Lao-tzu.

As far as the *Tao-Te-Ching* is concerned, it should be noted that this was not the original title. The text was given that name only during the later Han Dynasty or Hou Han (25-220 A.D.), that is, centuries after its compilation.

Ching as I have said, is the designation reserved to traditional texts. The more current translation of the text's title is "The Book (*Ching*) of the Way (*Tao*) and of its Virtue (*Te*)." I have changed this to "The Book of the Principle and of Its Action." This modification shows the fundamental ideas contained in the text, which is comprised of a metaphysic, an ethical system, a political doctrine, and finally, the elements of an esoteric doctrine of immortality.

In relation to pure metaphysics, the notion of *Tao* was known prior to Lao-tzu, it is found in all the Chinese schools of thought or orthodox teachings which are derived from the tradition of the *I-Ching*. Literally, as well as in the ideogram, *Tao* means "Way." It is the Way in which the All moves around. However, the term did not originally have a univocal meaning, since on the one hand it designated the "Great Principle" (although the main designation for it was "The Great One" or the "Great Vortex," *T'ai Ch'i*); on the other hand, it designated the sense of the world's course, the productive force and the immanent law of the manifestation of the Principle. In the title of Lao-tzu's work, these two aspects of the *Tao* are distinguished; the *Tao* is the Great Principle; its action, "virtue" or law, is the so-called *Te*. Such a distinction concerns the terms of a dynamic unity; and in this way, the characteristic Far Eastern *Weltanschauung* is found in the *Tao-Te-Ching*.

To make this clear, it must be remembered that the tradition in the East has had from the beginning a metaphysical and not a religious character. It ignored anthropomorphism and the humanization of the divine and instead focused on abstract and impersonal principles, which remained such even when they were described through material images taken from the world of nature. Thus, the Chinese spoke about *T'ien*, heaven, and not about "god." *T'ien* symbolizes transcendence. It was a figurative example of the Great Principle's infinite height, towering over and above the human dimension. Even when *T'ien* was personified in the State religion as the "Lord Above," (*Shang-Ti*), it never ceased to have an impersonal character; *Shang-ti* was described in relation to the above mentioned Great Principle with the title *Hang T'ien Shang-ti* (the highest Heaven, supreme god). This is the first characteristic of a Far Eastern *Weltanschauung*; it has a superhuman purity and traits which are essentially metaphysical. At the same time this *Weltanschauung* ignored the dualism of a supernatural world opposed to this concrete world. This fundamental unity has been recognized in the terms of what may be called an "immanent transcendence," despite the sense which it conveys, of what is infinitely far away and of what is non-human. The *Tao* of heaven is unreachable and, at the same time, tangible and really present within the "net" of phenomenal reality. In the *Tao-Te-Ching* this type of metaphysics is taken up, described in further detail and developed in an original way. Here the transcendent dimension of the Principle is again expressed through the specific employment of concepts such as emptiness, non-being, non-action, formless, or nameless, all of which indicate the supreme, detached essence of the Great One and of the Great Beginning. This Great Beginning is superior and prior to the "Being" of theistic and religious theologies.

Virtue (*Te*) is present as the immanent and acting aspect of the Principle. It is the power that unfolds the eternal manifestation of Perfection. This manifestation does not have a "creationist" character, in the theistic sense of the word; in other words, it is not related to a creating will and to a specific intent, but is part of the eternal, immutable and impersonal logic of the Divine.

In Lao-tzu, the term "way" refers to the concept of the One, which is not expressed in static terms, but in those of an eternal process, in which immanence and transcendence not only coexist, but influence each other and generate each other from the same one act. Here lies the characteristic feature of the doctrine found in the *Tao-Te-Ching*, which, if it could be reduced to the terms typical of mere intellectual speculation, would be mindful of some ideas of so-called European transcendental philosophy. Such a metaphysical situation is well expressed by Lao-tzu when he says that the Principle is (and that it produces by) "becoming empty." The image of a bellows (ch. 5) is used to designate the eternal act which, on the one hand, produces "emptiness," while on the other hand, gives being to the stream of forms, or to the "ten thousand beings." In several passages where the Principle is presented as a model, this idea is portrayed as an act of self-denial or as *not-being*, in order to be. It is almost an act of self-transcendence which, on the one hand, realizes the Principle as "emptiness," as absolute and as center; while, on the other hand, it exteriorizes and becomes free of substance in the course of an inexhaustible and impersonal process of giving, emanating and vivifying. Thus, it has been rightly suggested that in the context of Taoism, Lao-tzu's "virtue" is the means which the Principle itself needs in order to actualize itself.

I had mentioned earlier that what is given here, in a sort of metaphysical transparency, is what can be gathered from various confused myths, relative to the "sacrifices" of divine beings who originate creation.

There is found in this doctrine a mutual conditioning and a simultaneous presence of transcendence and immanence, both hyper-substantial non-being and being as the ultimate meaning of the Way of Heaven and also of the eternal development of the world. This is the origin of a view of non-being as an omnipresent substratum, or as the inner and essential dimension of being. Judging from yet another perspective, every thing, every being and every life-form is contained in the Way and in Perfection, and has never been outside of it. One Taoist teacher said: "If anything was, or existed outside the *Tao*, the *Tao* would not be the *Tao*." This doctrine originates the theories of spontaneity and of "natural" perfection, as well as the ethics of being in the Way, in virtue of just being what one is. On this matter there is a visible convergence of Taoism with Mahayana Buddhism, which upholds the transcendent identity of *samsara* (the contingent world) and *nirvana* (the Unconditioned), as two aspects of the same one reality. Because of this and other convergences (such as the one concerning the metaphysical notion of Emptiness, which is common to both schools of thought), an interesting symbiosis took place in China between Buddhism (imported in its Mahayana version at a time of a revival of Taoism) and Taoism. This symbiosis appears in various schools, from the ancient Chinese *Ch'an* to its derivatives, such as Japanese Zen. The above mentioned view about immanent transcendence and natural perfection was subsequently expressed by Zen, which claimed that every being has a Buddha nature and is "liberated," yet without being aware of it.

*　*　*　*　*

At this point I wish to discuss the Virtue (*te*) of the Principle, considered under its aspect of ordering power. It should be noted that in ancient Chinese language, *te* did not have a moral connotation (which it acquired only after the advent of Confucianism) but rather it evoked the power of action (during the Middle Ages in the Western world, mention was made of the "virtues" and "signatures" of a substance or of an element) and most of all, the power of magic. Magical power was designated both as *ling* and as *te*. In this sense the Chinese spoke about the five powers (*wu te*) which enabled the Chinese Dynasties to reign. This is also the case of *te* conceived as the virtue, or action, of Heaven. The teaching of the *Tao-Te-Ching* is that, due to the real presence of transcendence within immanence, a higher order is realized in the world in an invisible and spontaneous way that is somewhat magical and typical of "non-acting" Taoism. The expression "non-acting" means that what is taking place is not direct divine intervention in the course of human events, with regulating and moralizing purposes, as in the case of the theistic theology of Providence, but rather a superior influence, which is not confined to specific ends or intentions, and which is uncaring about individual existences (without "any wish to be benevolent," says Lao-tzu.[2] While allowing freedom to things and beings, this influence combines the totality of events in such a way as to mirror the Great Unity and Perfection. The Taoist images employed are those of the net of Heaven, which has large meshes, but from which nothing ever escapes (*Tao-Te-Ching*, ch. 73), or that of the bottom of a great valley which does not act, but toward which all the waters running on the slopes, irresistibly descend and converge; this character possesses the Virtue (*te*) of the Principle. There are also some sayings of Chuang-tzu, which further exemplify this notion: "It is the *Tao* that overspreads and sustains all things. How great It is in Its overflowing influence!" [3]

Generally speaking, or in non-metaphysical terms, *te* is also conceived as a "power of presence." Beings and things can be centers of *te*, especially "real men" and "transcendent men." They are said to "act without acting," mirroring in this the *Tao*. In other words, they exercise in an impersonal way an irresistible and efficacious influence, just in virtue of their presence, without performing any action or developing any particular intention, hence the passage from the metaphysics of *Tao* to the ethics and politics of the *Tao*. When the previously mentioned ideas are added to this particular view of *te*, the overall cosmic picture which emerges is one of an inexhaustible process of flowing and generating, which is permeated by "Emptiness," and one of an eternal and immutable law which operates, through the magic of Virtue, within every change, directing without touching, dominating without imposing itself, bringing to completion without doing anything in particular. In this inscrutable action there is the principle of the actions and subsequent reactions, which was already described in the metaphysics of the *I-Ching*. I will mention here two instances, as far as Taoist metaphysic is concerned. The first instance concerns the traditional theory of the metaphysical Dyad, which was already outlined in the teachings of the *I-Ching* as well in the doctrine of the *yin* and *yang*. The manifestation of the *Tao* unfolds through the alternated interplay of *yin* and *yang*, which are opposite and yet complementary and inseparable multivalent principles. They are the eternal masculine and feminine; the active and the passive; Heaven (in a limited sense) and earth; the luminous and the dark; the creative and the receptive, and so on. The *I-Ching* had reduced the structure of every process, being and phenomenon to various dynamic combinations of these two powers or qualities, immortalizing them in the system of tri-grams and esa-grams, which are signs composed of *yin* and *yang*. It is through the *yin* and *yang* that the Way of Heaven operates. A particular idea which often recurs in the *Tao-Te-Ching* is that of the conversion of opposites. There cannot be an indefinite increase or development of a given quality, whether it be *yin* or *yang*; once a quality reaches its peak, it encounters the limit beyond which the overturning, or the conversion into the opposite quality occurs. For instance, a peace protracted beyond the limit generates disorder and war; an extreme disorder produces order; the ascent is followed by a descent (a popular proverb says: "When the moon is full, it begins to set.") In this system, the invisible, regulating, rectifying and compensating action of the Virtue of the Great Principle is manifested, as if in an immense circular process.

The second instance concerns the notion of mutation, *yi*, in which, according to both *I-Ching* and Taoism, the intimations of production, creation, development and becoming are summed up. Beings and things appear, become and disappear, in virtue of a "change of state." In everything that happens, rises and declines (in birth, life and death), there are only changes of state. This is a fundamental view in the metaphysical systems of the East. In the Principle, the potentialities of being are present in a pre-formal state. Through the eternal power of the One (equated in this aspect to the feminine functions of bringing to life by generating, of feeding and of nourishing), these potentialities assume a formal state (as we shall see, "corporeity" is a synonym of this state) and thus enter into the stream of transformations. They could remain in this stream, caught up in an undetermined situation, analogous to that of the Hindu *samsara* and of the Hellenic *kuklos tes geneseos* (the cycle of generation), if attachment to a form still persists in them. This situation, though, should not be understood in terms of reincarnation, namely as a necessary and repeated reappearance in the human condition, but rather as "transmigration," since being a human being is just an episode in the chain of transformations. In that event, these potentialities undergo a crisis of discontinuity caused by the various changes of state, namely by the "going out" (being born) and by the "coming back" (dying). These crises can be overcome when these potentialities separate themselves from the formal condition and become integrated into that Transcendence which is present and active in Immanence. When this occurs, they become "men of *Tao*" or "men of the Way." In technical language, according to the etymology of the word, "transformation" ("to go beyond the form") corresponds to the second case; transformations of the first case, taking place in a "horizontal" sense, in a succession or in a cyclical pattern, are mere "changes of state" and metaphysically irrelevant. With the exception of what is proper to the domain of esoteric Taoism, to which I will refer later on, and from the absolute point of view of this doctrine, not unlike Vedanta and Mahayana (Scotus Erigena and Meister Eckhart may be considered their Western counterparts), the difference between these two conditions consists in a pure matter of consciousness. It has already been said that according to this point of view, nothing is ever outside the Way or the Great Perfection. In the *Tao-Te-Ching* this is expressed by the saying "Great, it passes on. Passing on, it becomes remote. Having become remote, it returns."[4] In the stream of forms, the end and the beginning get mixed up and, as another text suggests, "They become illuminated by a great light."

Therefore, what according to the men of Tao must be the way to follow, derives immediately from metaphysics. This way consists in excluding any extroverted action which proceeds from the peripheral center, as well as any action aimed at strengthening and at expanding this peripheral center, constituted by the exteriorized formal existence (the empirical, individual Ego); this is done in order to *be* and in order to *act* while remaining within the realm of transcendence. Transcendence is the metaphysical "empty" dimension, always present beyond all changes of state, where one can find the true root and the essential, indestructible center of all things.

*　　*　　*　　*　　*

Let us now consider the domain of personal realization as contemplated in the *Tao-Te-Ching*. At the heart of the text is the figure of him who is called *cheng-jen*. Over and over, Lao-tzu describes the type, the behavior, the nobility and the way of

13

acting of this figure. The dependence of ethics on metaphysics is here very evident. In the *Tao-Te-Ching* what comes first are the metaphysical *enunciates*; then, through the conjunction "so" or through another analogy, what is proper to the *cheng-jen* is evidentiated. This being is patterned after the Way, not after a human moral ideal. While in Lao-tzu the prevalent term is *cheng-jen*, in Taoism we encounter the other terms *chen-jen* and *shen-jen*, which identify a being often identified with the first one. It is necessary at this point to find a term best suited to translate *cheng-jen*. The terms which are most often used by translators, the "Saint" or the "Wise Man," should be excluded. While the term "Wise Man" is linguistically correct, it still evokes a poetical and philosophical image. In the West, it evokes figures such as Socrates, Plato or Boethius, even though these types are still very different from the Taoist ideal. Besides, the *cheng-jen* as "Wise Man" is closer to the ideal of exoteric Confucianism, which is ideologically very distant from Taoism. The term "Saint" is even less suited because of its moral and religious connotation, which is absolutely lacking in the *sheng-jen*. The *sheng-jen* also lacks the emotive, devotional and ecstatic attitude which is typical of the mystic. Finally, because of an analogous reason, namely because of a possible reference to a merely moral fulfillment within the human condition, I have avoided a third term, namely the "Perfect Man," although I have used it myself on other occasions. On the basis of the above-mentioned relationship between the Taoist designations, I have employed the term "real man" or "realized man" to translate *cheng-jen*. A higher dimension, that of the "transcendent man" (*shen-jen*) must likewise be referred to the "real man," despite the difference existing between the "real man" and the "transcendent man," which Guenon has well documented (*The Great Triad*, Paris, 1946, ch. 18). If the term was not too technical, one could properly speak of "follower" in an initiatory sense, rather than of Saint, Philosopher, Mystic or Wise Man, since, as far as his ontological status is concerned, this is what a *cheng-jen* is. Besides, this is helpful in not losing sight of a certain magical quality which is present in this type of person. The "Men of *Tao*" (*tao-che*) were also called, in the beginning of the Christian era, *fang-shi*, a term which alludes to this magical quality. It is a common opinion that possession of *Tao* bestows a magical force; thus the masters are called *te-jen*, namely "Men of *te*" (as in power). However, the term "initiate" is too specific, therefore I have preferred to render *sheng-jen* with "real man."

*　*　*　*　*

"Real man" is one who reproduces in himself the metaphysical law of *Tao*. This kind of man, in order to be, chooses not to be. By denying himself, he asserts himself; by disappearing, he remains at the center; by being empty, he is full; by hiding, he shines forward; by lowering himself, he stands out. All this happens in an impersonal and non-sentimental way, which is very different from the spirit informing an analogous ethics found outside Taoist China, e.g., in the Christian religion. The fundamental theme is also expressed by the technical expression "preserving the One" (*chen-yi*) or "preserving the Essence" (*tsing*). Man becomes lost because he misplaces the original power outside of himself, thus concretizing the Ego, super-saturating it, identifying with or exciting "life," feeding the attachment to that portion of life which he has "stolen" and to which now he desperately clings. The path of perfection, or integration, consists in just the opposite; to de-saturate, to let go, to become naked, more simple, not acting, to leave the radius and to go back to the source. Just like in the Tao, in man too there is a continuous, free flow of life which promotes the essential detachment, transcendence, and permanence in what is immaterial and elusive. This flow dissolves the existential entanglement into a superior spontaneity and into a calm self-control. In the human world, this is the "higher virtue" opposed to the "lower virtue," which consists in acting and in striving with the mere aid of the limited human strength and of the illusory center constituted by the individual Ego, while being cut off from the Way.

Therefore, it becomes evident how absurd it is to label Lao-tzu's doctrine as quietist. It is a total blunder on the part of a Chinese scholar to say, like many Europeans do, that the "non-acting" which is required to reach the "conformity of *Tao*" is the "weakness manifested by non-desiring, by not knowing, by being satisfied with little, by humility, and so on." (P. Siao Shi Tu's translation of the *Tao-Te-Ching*, Bari, Italy, 1947, p. 20)

If anything, this is not an example of quietism but of the more purified and subtler doctrine of the "superman." Misunderstandings of this kind find disgraceful expressions in the terms in which several passages of the *Tao-Te-Ching* have been rendered, since it is inferred from them a very mediocre wisdom applied to the social and political realms. Due to the multiple meanings found in a language based on ideograms, anyone can find in similar passages a meaning which reflects one's spiritual mediocrity, but it must be remembered that the essential meaning is almost always expressed in inner and spiritual terms. The Taoist norms are meant to regulate the deepest and transcendent inner life, and not the external, social conduct. The ethics of Lao-tzu is substantially an initiatory ethics.

As far as the Taoist notion of "non acting" (*wu wei*) is concerned, its positive counterpart is "acting without acting" (*wei-wu-wei*). As I have said, *wu wei* only means non-action on the part of the peripheral Ego and the exclusion of "doing" in a direct and material sense as well as of the employment of the exteriorized power. This *wu wei* is the condition for the manifestation of a superior kind of action, which is *wei-wu-wei* precisely. *Wei-wu-wei* comes into play as "Heaven's" action, in its characteristic of *te*, which is the invisible spiritual power which brings everything to fulfillment, irresistibly but also "naturally." Through paradoxical formulations, Lao-tzu repeatedly emphasizes this concept: detachment, abandonment, not-wanting, not acting, are practiced in order to free real action, which is identical to the Way. Chuang-tzu said: "The Human and the Heavenly are one and the same.... That man can not have Heaven is owing to the limitation of his own nature."[5] "Being thus in its nature; unseen it causes harmony; unmoving it transforms; unmoved it perfects."[6]

In this context we can observe the evident absurdity, which so many translators or commentators are guilty of, to see in Taoist precepts relative to the individual and to society some kind of "return to nature," yielding the promise of natural goodness and spontaneity, almost as if Lao-tzu was a Rousseau twenty-three centuries before his time, writing the apology of the "good savage" and the corresponding indictment of the "corrupting influence of society," typical of the European eighteenth century. It is true that in Taoism, the denial of "culture" (the external knowledge; rationalism; the artificial social system; the small-minded, busy-bodied political wisdom; the zeal to "enlighten the people"; and everything else, including even the study of books written on the *Tao*, which Chuang-tzu called "the Ancients' excrements") is even more radical than in other ideologies similar to that of Rousseau. However, the counterpart to "culture" in this context is something that has nothing to do with nature and with spontaneity, as they have been conceived in the West.

Just as in some Far Eastern texts, the term "natural" very often is synonymous of "heavenly," likewise "nature" was conceived as the Way itself, in its sensible form, namely the elusive, incorporeal, heavenly order in act: "What Heaven has disposed and sealed is called the inborn nature."[7]

Thus, the spontaneity being mentioned, which operates everything as long as one does not act and does not interfere with it, is the transcendental spontaneity of Heaven's Way. The Taoist "original spontaneity" (*p'uo*) is not a trite, primitivist and almost animal-like innocence, but is the state that was hinted about in other traditions through the myth of the golden age or other myths concerning the origins. This state was characterized by the naturality of the supernatural and by the supernaturality of the natural. It should be noted that in both Lao-tzu and in older orthodox texts, up to the one attributed to the legendary Fo-hi (who reigned from 3468 B.C. onward), mention is made of an even older age, the way of which should be revived. (Confucius allegedly said about Lao-tzu: "This man pretends to practice the wisdom of the primordial age.") According to the Taoist saying: "It is necessary that the heavenly element predominate in order for the action to be conformed to the original perfection," the heavenly element is a synonym of the natural element, and it is set against the human element. Therefore a Westerner must realize that what he may be inclined to see as "naturalism," is rather a *Weltanschauung* proper to a humanity which was somehow still connected to the origins, or to "super-nature" in a direct and existential fashion, and not through theories, revelations or religions strictly speaking (*religio* from *religare*, namely to reconnect what was already separated), as it was the case in later stages or cycles of civilization.

This is the key to understand the true nature of Far Eastern spirituality, as well as its specific expressions such as the artistic ones (e.g., painting, in which "nature" is portrayed in an evanescent way, hinting to an ethereal, metaphysical "emptiness"). This is also the key to explain the absence, in that ancient spirituality and in what has been preserved of it, of the ascetical element, strictly speaking, namely of effort, mortification and violent overcoming. Finally, it is the key to understand the above-mentioned and often misunderstood aspects of the *Tao-Te-Ching* concerning non-action.

In reference to the "real man," not-acting characterizes he who escapes the interplay of actions and ensuing reactions, in order to act instead on the invisible and pre-formal plane of those causes and processes which are about to come into being. In relation to this, one finds in the *Tao-Te-Ching* the fundamental idea present in the *I-Ching*, considered as a book of "oracles," namely the idea of preventing the occurrence of events and of situations, and of acting instead on what is still in the process of becoming, on the basis of the knowledge of the "images" of what takes place both in heaven and on earth. The tradition of the *I-Ching* had already defined the type of the one who, by the employment of this knowledge, is capable of preventing, controlling and directing the interplay of actions and reactions of the *yin* and *yang* in the world of forms and of beings, beyond the immobile and impersonal principle, of which he embodies the nature. Therefore, this aspect of Taoist "not-acting" may be characterized as the choice of not putting oneself on the same plane of the forces or things which one is trying to control. By analogy, a comparison with Japanese wrestling has rightly been suggested, in which "one should never oppose strength with strength; instead, one should throw down the opponent by turning his own strength against him (C. Puini)." The "real man" *does not act* (he gives in, he withdraws, he bends) in order to gain the initiative in what constitutes true action. In reference to this, Lao-tzu talked about winning without fighting, about tying without using knots, about drawing things to oneself without calling out for them or moving in their direction. In a more specific way, a reference can be made to magic, when *wu-wei* is compared to the imperceptible action on what is still "weak" or "soft," in order to prevent further developments, arrest them and lead them in a chosen direction, which appears to be natural to profane eyes. In this sense, in the *Tao-Te-Ching*, it is said that the weak prevails on the strong, what is small over what is bigger, what is soft before what is hard. The simile of water is employed, which takes on various forms, but which can erode what is hard and rigid.

Leaving aside the doctrine of *wu-wei*, there are two possible ways in which the *sheng-jen* can appear. The first way is as an "obscure initiate." Sse Ma Chien relates: "Lao-tzu's school's main concern was to remain inconspicuous and not make a name for itself by becoming famous." According to another saying: "A true Sage does not leave tracks." The *sheng-jen* can externally be identified to the common man, even to the contemptible man, appearing to lack knowledge, ability, practical sense, culture or ambitions, as one who is transported by the worldly stream, avoiding to stand up, to be conspicuous. This happens because of some kind of reflection, in his empirical humanity and in his behavior, of his keeping to himself, without externalizing anything. This impenetrable type of initiate may seem, and to a certain extent it truly is, very Far Eastern; however, it is still found in other traditions, such as Mahayana Buddhism, Islam and, in a later period, in the Western Hermetic tradition and in Rosicrucianism. In Lao-tzu the description of the "real man" in such a cryptic form includes a vein of antinomism, namely of contempt for current values and norms, of the so-called "little virtue" and of what is related to the regulated social life. In Sufism mention is made of the *malamatiyah*, the "blameworthy ones," who enjoy a higher, yet unknown dignity. In a Tibetan legend, Naropa cannot find his master Tilopa, because every time he encounters him he cannot recognize him as the person doing something which he, Naropa, considers reproachable. In Islam one finds the type of the *majadhib*, who are initiates who have operated a split, whereby their transcendental development has no consequences for their inferior and human dimension, which is abandoned to itself.

In the <u>Tao-Te-Ching</u> there are suggestive characterizations of this type of person, which are expressed in a well-known and paradoxical style. Such a one cannot be treated familiarly or distantly; he is beyond all consideration of nobility or meanness (ch 56). Men resort to him and find rest, peace and the feeling of ease (ch. 35). He is straight among the crooked; full among the empty; new among the worn out (ch. 22). He wears a poor garb of hair cloth, while he carries his signet of jade in his bosom (ch. 70). He is like water, without form, elusive. Wishing to be above men, he puts himself beneath them with his words, and wishing to be before men he places his person behind them. Though he is an elusive being, if he chooses to act, his action reaches the intended goal despite any resistance encountered, precisely because he belongs to another plane. One can even find here the magical trait of physical invulnerability, which is almost a chrism, and a tangible and symbolic sign of his transcendent detachment, which creates a different ontological <u>status</u> (ch. 50). This is what Chuang-tzu had to say on the matter: "He has the form of a man, and therefore he is a man. Being without the passions and desires of men, their approving and disapproving are not to be found in him. How insignificant and small is the body by which he belongs to humanity! How grand and great is he in the unique perfection of his Heavenly nature!"[8] On the contrary, the second way in which the Taoist *sheng-jen* can appear, is in situations in which a given structure of society and of civilization facilitates the correspondence of the inner and secret quality with an external authority and dignity, in the exercise of the visible functions proper of a leader, an ordering figure and a sovereign. In this case, the figure of the *cheng-jen* becomes confused with *Wang Ti*, the "Son of Heaven," found in the Chinese Dynasties.

There is a second possibility. In the *Tao-Te-Ching* the references to the latter type of "real man" are not less numerous than those referring to the former type. This leads us to consider the third aspect of Taoist teachings, namely the application of the *Tao's* metaphysics to the political realm.

*   *   *   *   *

Lao-tzu's doctrine is intrinsically not "mystical" at all, and this is especially true if one considers his constantly using the Way in reference to him who has the task of ordering society and of being the center or the pole of the worldly forces. In Lao-tzu, this regent figure is never set against the figure representative of an escapist and abstract spirituality. Even in this instance Lao-tzu remains strictly within the parameters of the primordial Chinese tradition, which was a tradition of unity, not only on a purely metaphysical plane, but on the political plane as well. This tradition ignored the division of the two powers (spiritual and political authority), and, beginning with *I-Ching* and with its commentators, it associated the teachings of the transcendent wisdom to the figures of emperors and princes (Fo-hi, the "Yellow Emperor," Wen-Wang, and so on), and not to a separated priestly or "philosophical" class. The sovereigns were the custodians of doctrine. The Chinese were inclined to believe that leadership and the function of *regere* according to "Heaven's mandate," were the natural and eminent prerogatives of he who possessed knowledge and who played the role of a "royal man" or of a "transcendent man." In this context, the Oriental notion of the so-called Great Triad (Heaven, Earth and Man) acquires a fundamental meaning. Man, conceived as the mediator between Heaven and Earth, is essentially man as sovereign, and the sovereign as a "real man." This teaching,

18

which is also shared by Confucianism (see *Chung Yung*, ch. 22) is expressed in identical terms in the *Tao-Te-Ching* (ch. 25). The eminent function of the sovereign is to keep the communication line between Heaven and Earth open.

The essence of Taoist ethics and politics is the imitation of the Principle, which includes not-acting as well. Up to 1912, when the ancient regime collapsed, the expression *wu-wei* (not-acting) was written on the Chinese imperial throne. It is necessary to emphasize that, in this instance as well, the misunderstanding incurred by the majority of Lao-tzu's translators and commentators, was not inferior to that which they demonstrated when they talked about Taoist "pietism" and "passivity" as an individual ideal. The precept of excluding from government the exercise of strength and of coercion and of not intervening with a heavy hand in the delicate and complex mechanism of social forces; the idea that overdoing, over-organizing, rationalizing, legislating and imposing precepts regulating "social relationships" and virtue, eventually lead to the opposite effects which are desired; the principle according to which everything must organize itself, and that only natural developments and the maturation of effects from given causes must be propitiated, so that the political *optimum* must be seen where the "ten thousand beings" and "everything under the sun" are almost unaware of being ruled and directed; all this, in the *Tao-Te-Ching*, does not bear any resemblance to political absenteeism or to an utopian society which evokes Rousseau and the denial of authority or higher power, and thus, the very idea of the State. This misinterpretation on the part of modern Europeans is almost inevitable, since they no longer have a sense of the political context or the fundamental values proper to primordial and traditional regimes. To have understood the true meaning of Taoist metaphysics and of the way of being of "real men," is to realize that what is at stake is something radically different. First of all, the idea of the State is eminently upheld since, as I have already said, the State or the empire is even conceived as the earthly image of the Way, and almost as its emanation. The attribute "Olympian" well characterizes the political regime that conforms to the *Tao*, provided that it is taken in the right sense and the norm followed by the ruler coincides with the norm dictated by personal ethics. This norm consists in detachment, not-acting as an individual in order to exercise an action which despite being subtle, invisible and immaterial is not any less real, but on the contrary, more efficient than the action in which strength, any "activist" intervention and coercion are employed. The ruler must represent the "unwobbling pivot" (as per in Confucius' own view). Just as the Great Principle, he is absent, but because of that he is supremely and impersonally present. He exercises "Heaven's action" by acting only in virtue of his presence, of his being there as a "real man," of his transcendence.

This is the direct application of the doctrine of the Great Triad, in which man is conceived as a third power between Heaven and earth, in a context which may appear unusual only if one loses sight of the convergence, in this tradition, of the political and the sacred functions. A similar idea was also found in the West, (though limited to the sacred domain), and specifically in the function of the pontiff, according to the etymology of the word ("maker of bridges"): pontiffs were those beings who were conceived as mediators, and as ways employed to spread a higher influence in the human world or even as impersonal centers of such an influence (in Taoist terms, of *te*). The idea of "active immobility" was also known in Aristotelian philosophy, as well as in Oriental traditions (it is reflected, for instance, in Hindu deities of a *Purushic* type). Taoism merely refers this order of ideas to the *cheng-jen* as the sovereign.

Thus, what is essential in the notion of *regere*, are not specific material actions, or "doing," or human cares and concerns, but to possess and to nourish *te*, Virtue. This is accomplished by becoming united with the Principle; by destroying every particularism and irrational impulse within one's self; and by conforming one's nature to the nature of the "center." Then the sovereign will radiate an influence which resolves tensions, imperceptibly and invisibly moderates and rearranges the interplay of forces in the general equilibrium, wins without fighting, bends without using violence, rectifies and propitiates a climate in which everything can develop in a "natural" way, conforming to the Way in such a degree as to "resemble the primordial state."

Two conditions are necessary for the right function of this influence. The first, at a higher level, is precisely the sovereign's not-acting and impersonal impassability. He must be detached from every human feeling, and from any mania of *grandeur*. He must remain neutral before both good and evil, just as the *Tao* is, from a metaphysical point of view. In fact, any departure from such a neutrality or centrality, would paralyze Virtue and produce chaos around him as an immediate repercussion. The second condition, at a lower level, is that the "ten thousand beings," namely the people, must retain the "primordial simplicity." In other words, they should not wish to be what they are not and they should remain faithful to their own nature. Also, they should implement, each one at his/her own level, and at the best of his/her abilities, the Taoist ethic which shuns extroversion, individualism, frantic pursuit of unnatural goals, greed, lack of equilibrium and excess. When these conditions are met, "Heaven's action" will be felt in a positive way, through the previously described atmosphere, in which positive dispositions will be inclined to develop freely and naturally. This action will also be felt in a negative way by leading back again to the right order those forces which tend to avoid, through the interplay of actions and ensuing reactions, the convergence of paths and of destinies, as well as the law of the conversion of the opposites, whenever these forces reach their limit. Acting without acting in the context of an Olympian and supernatural view of royalty is the function of the Taoist ruler, as it is highlighted in the *Tao-Te-Ching* and evidentiated in two other teachers, Lieh-tzu and Chuang-tzu.

It must be admitted that of the two conditions, the latter is utopian only when it is referring to the orientation of contemporary mankind. The Western world knew, even shortly after the Middle Ages, the faithfulness of large sectors of society to their own state in life and to their own nature. This was the basis of the stability of the *ancien regime*. In Europe there were traces of "Olympian royalty" wherever the temporal power did not dissociate itself from spiritual authority and wherever the monarchies of divine right enjoyed an intrinsic prestige, a symbolic character and a mysticism of their own. However, China itself, during the first centuries of Taoism, was far from reflecting the social milieu envisioned by that political principle of not-acting which was reaffirmed in Lao-tzu's doctrine. Thus, Confucianism followed yet another path, namely that of a social and human "corrective surgery" which was based more on normative principles than on the original spontaneity envisioned by Taoism. The so-called School of Law of Han Fei-tzu demonstrated a healthy realism by combining the two needs, and by interpreting the Taoist ideas in the following fashion: what is needed first are drastic measures aimed at punishing any transgression and any excess, in order to bring back the individuals and the masses to the natural state; only then the political principle of not-acting should be applied in order to produce natural and free developments which are supported by a supernatural influence. On the contrary, in Lao-tzu, the principles of metaphysically oriented political views, of Olympian sovereignty and of an invisible and ordained from above action, know no compromise or attenuation, since they strictly adhere to the pure doctrine of the origins. This is true even when the stages of the descent and the involution of the political principle are known and described in detail. This involution leads eventually to a situation where the ruler is only feared, and, in the last stage, despised and hated.

What has been said so far leads to some final considerations on the fourth and last aspect of the doctrine of *Tao*, concerning the initiatory notion of immortality.

Among sinologists, the current opinion is that after the time of Lao-tzu, Lieh-tzu and Chuang-tzu, Taoism became corrupted and degenerated. Having ceased to be "philosophical and mystical," it was transformed into a religion which absorbed the most primitive and spurious popular beliefs on the one hand and on the other, it generated a body of doctrines and superstitious practices associated with alchemy and magic, based on a quest for "physical immortality" and thaumaturgical powers.

This is only partially true. Having ascertained that the essential nucleus of the doctrine of the origins did not have a "philosophical and mystical" character but rather a metaphysical character (which is not quite the same thing), it is certainly possible to notice in the history of Taoism, the same process of degeneration undergone by Buddhism, which in the beginning, (as a doctrine of the awakening and enlightening), had an exclusively initiatory character. For both Taoism and Buddhism, this was the fatal consequence of spreading geographically and growing in popularity. As early as the first centuries of this era, Taoism was transformed into a religion which attracted the popular masses, reaching its *apogee* between the fourth and sixth centuries A.D. under six Dynasties. It even gave rise to a political movement; the revolt of the so-called "Yellow Turbans" overturned the rule of the Han dynasty during the second half of the II century A.D. In such a popular religion, the abstract metaphysical principles and stages of inner experience of the original doctrine were transformed into a number of deities, spirits and entities which increasingly populated a fantastic and baroque pantheon, analogous to that of Mahayana Buddhism. Like Buddha, Lao-tzu was deified. The constant forms found in it, typical of mere religion, became prevalent. These forms consist in turning to the gods in order to receive salvation; in the need of an external spiritual help; in faith; in devotion; and in a cult endowed with collective as well as individual rituals and ceremonies. All of this can be characterized as a regression, in which Taoism radically departed from the spirit of the early days.

After Taoism became a popular religion and an exoteric system, and after it partially mingled with Buddhism, it faced a rapid decline and it survived only as a cult practiced by monks or as the practice of wizards. Eventually it became contemptible in the eyes of the Chinese intellectual elites.

It is a different story when it comes to what has been mistakenly considered a body of superstitious and magical techniques, leading to the achievement of "physical immortality." This is not a degeneration but rather the operative and esoteric dimension of Taoism. In this dimension a doctrine took a specific form, and this doctrine, in its essence, not only conformed to tradition, but is the basis of everything which is considered initiation, even outside the East. The misunderstanding arose due to the fact the majority of the people learned about these aspects of Taoism only when they became degenerated and when they were appropriated by coteries and by sects which could not expound their true meaning. Eventually the doctrines themselves were attributed the problematic and distorted characteristics found in later developments. However, even some sinologists had to acknowledge that as early as in the writings of the Taoist founding figures, there are traces of the initiatory doctrine of immortality, and that this doctrine is not, as it is claimed by many scholars, a more recent and spurious development, based on distorted and fanciful interpretations of the *Tao-Te-Ching* and other scriptures. It is true that in such ancient texts one can only find cryptic hints to this doctrine, but, as I have already remarked, in Lao-tzu and in other figures one should not merely see isolated individuals expounding personal insights, but rather the representatives of schools of thought and initiatory chains which preserved the integral doctrine *ab antiquo*. It is necessary to refer to the latter, when some Taoist traditions mention the "real immortals who have achieved the *Tao*," and who transmit only among themselves, orally, the secret teaching concerning initiatory practices, solemnly swearing never to divulge them to others.

Having said that, I wish to give a brief overview of this issue, even though one finds valid reference to it, not so much in the *Tao-Te-Ching*, but rather in the tradition to which this text belongs, and which was popularized through various distortions.

In order to make sense of the doctrine of immortality, which is shared by Taoism and by other Eastern and Western initiatory schools, it will be useful to compare it with the religious views expressed by Christianity as a way of example. According to Christianity every soul is immortal; immortality is the soul's substance and it is taken for granted. The issue, in Christianity, is not whether the soul survives death, but only the way in which it will survive, namely whether it will obtain bliss in Heaven or suffer the eternal punishments of hell. Thus, the believer's main concern is not to escape death, but to avoid the fate of hell and obtain the rewards of Heaven for his immortal soul. This capsules the Christian conception of "salvation" (*salus*).

The initiatory doctrine views the matter in quite a different way: the problem is not *how* the soul survives, but *whether* it survives. The real alternative is between survival and non-survival, since survival and immortality are not taken for granted, but are seen as a simple and unusual outcome. According to Taoism, almost everybody is inscribed in the Book of Death. In some exceptional cases the Ruler of Destiny cancels a person's name from this book and inscribes it instead in the Book of Life, which contains the names of the Immortals. It would be easy to indicate the correspondences of this anti-democratic view of immortality with other traditions which express it in the inner content of their own myths. It suffices to mention the idea found in ancient Hellas of the double fate incurred by the "heroes" who are destined to attain the almost Olympian seats of the immortal gods, and by the *oi polloi*. But in esoteric Taoism, besides the doctrine, there is a body of techniques which has to be applied in order to obtain the privilege of immortality, by inducing a change of state, namely the previously mentioned "transformation."

A second difference between initiatory doctrine and religious exotericism is that while according to the latter the soul enjoys immortality upon becoming detached from the body, Taoism upholds the seemingly bizarre idea that immortality should be "constructed" *in* the body and through the transformation *of* the body. This idea, which is also found in other initiatory and mystery teachings, finds a favorable context in the metaphysics of the Far East. This metaphysics, beginning with the comments found in the *I-Ching*, has ignored the dualism of body and soul, of spirit and matter. In this context, birth has been conceived as the passage of a being from the invisible and formless state to the visible and formal state. Corporeality has likewise been conceived merely as existence in a form, or as an exteriorized existence. The latter has been explained as the coalescence, or bonding, of the spiritual element. In order to explain the ensuing change of state, some symbolic and corporeal images have been provided, such as that of the fixing of spirits or "breath" or the coagulation of the subtle and ethereal substance (*khi*). In its deepest meaning, the fixing consists in the identification of being with a formal existence. The formal, exteriorized existence is then caught up in the current of transformations, and thus becomes subject to the crises proper to every change of state, as well as to the process of exiting a state (dying) in order to enter a new one (being born). It seems natural that this crisis can have destructive consequences for those who have become fixed in a form, that is, in the bodily state. Having failed to preserve and having "dissipated" the sense of the One or the Essence, such a being cannot survive, but will repeatedly "enter" and "exit" the life stream, though nothing permanent will survive. According to Taoism, his being, as an individual, will disintegrate. At the moment of death, since the metaphysical principle is clouded, the various forces (portrayed as many entities residing in the body) kept together in the bodily organism, and in general, in the human personality, become free and cease to supply a foundation to consciousness and to the sense of continuity of the individual Ego.

This is an extremely realistic, and the digressive background on which the esoteric doctrine of immortality is articulated. According to this doctrine, immortality must be elaborated in the body while one is alive (dying before one's time is thus considered a disgraceful circumstance), on the basis of an ontological and existential transformation taking place in the condition of the formal existence. Immortality does not mean physically escaping death, but rather avoiding altogether the crisis which, in the case of ordinary people, is connected to the transformation or change of state (*hua*). Thus, the legendary sovereign Yan-Shang was said to be "the only one who was not transformed in the course of the universal transformation."

*　*　*　*　*

It is not necessary at this point to focus on details. The techniques employed in Taoism aim at limiting the extroverted tendency to identify with and to become dissipated into the essence of life (in the *Tao-Te-Ching* there are several passages susceptible to take on such an operative meaning) and also to generate and to nourish what is called "the immortal embryo" or the "mysterious embryo," by dissolving the coagulation of formal existence. This could be expressed with the dualistic Western conceptual framework, by saying that the "body" is transformed into "spirit," or that "body" and "spirit" become one thing in virtue of the reintegration into the Principle. Maspero, a celebrated sinologist, quoted the following passage taken from the *Yun-ki ts'i-ts'ien*:

> *The body becomes penetrated by the Tao and thus becomes one with the spirit; he whose body and spirit are united and form one thing, is called "divine man" (shen-jen). In that instance, the nature of spirit is empty and sublimated, and its substance is not destroyed during the transformation. Since the body is similar in all things to life, there is no longer any life or death... to go on living or to die is up to the individual; one comes and goes without interval... The material body, having been transformed, is identical to the spirit; the melted spirit becomes subtle and forms one thing with the Tao.*[9]

"Melted" and "to melt" are technical terms of operative Taoism, which are synonymous of "de-coagulate," in the same sense in which a metal goes from the solid state to a fluid one (fusion), when fire is employed as an agent.

The act of "freezing" in a given form, is overcome; only then, death is turned into a mere change of state, which does not affect the essence. Everything becomes alive in the current of the primordial vital fluid (*khi*) with which contact has been re-established. This process is not conceived in abstract and spiritual terms. During the fusion, the many powers of the psycho-physical connection, which otherwise would become dissociated and freed, are integrated and resumed in the essential One. Hence the specifically Taoist notion, which is found in the various "biographies of real men who have embodied the *Tao*," of the fusion or solution of the corpse (*she kiai*). The Taoist initiate, when dying, does not leave a body behind. In his tomb, there is only to be found a symbolic sword or scepter. This is the mark of the "Men of *Tao*," who are superior beings, and who are said to be "Immortals."

They are immortal not in the sense that they will live forever as human beings, but in the sense that they only die in appearance, because they have been integrated without any residue in the central principle which is superior to both life and death. Therefore, the true meaning of the Taoist notion of "bodily immortality" is that the form which has been integrated in the pre-formal, is now transferred into the primordial and not-exteriorized condition, which is not subject to the flux of modifications and changes. By analogy, it can be said that an "immortal body" has been generated. In this context, it is possible to talk about "pure forms," in an analogous sense to that which was given by scholasticism to this term. Laymen or semi-initiates, who could not understand the teaching in these metaphysical and esoteric terms, assumed it in a coarse and superstitious way, and attempted to develop techniques that could eliminate old age and illness, as well as indefinitely prolong physical existence. Since the doctrine of immortality degenerated into superstitious forms, it generated gross misunderstandings. However, it should not be excluded that certain extra-normal possibilities may trickle down from spiritual realization into human existence, and that these possibilities may have been cultivated by some schools.

Westerners are also likely to misunderstand the terminology characterizing this doctrine, since the expression which is employed most of the times is *ch'ang-sheng*, which literally means "long life," even though this expression refers to an endless and continuous life, and by extension, to immortality (I mentioned earlier that "old age" in China had a similar meaning, hence the attribute "old," which was bestowed on various deities and on Lao-tzu himself). It is easy, therefore, to be misled into thinking that the Teachers exclusively focused on longevity and on the preparation of an elixir of long life. An even worse distortion is found in religious Taoism, in which the esoteric doctrine of immortality generated the myth according to which the believer, after death, reclaims his body, leaves the sepulchre, and goes on to dwell in the immortals' heavenly abodes. This is the exact correspondence of the unsophisticated exoteric Christian doctrine of the "resurrection of the flesh," which was developed in the same way, namely through an obtuse interpretation of some teachings of the Mystery Religions, which were borrowed by early Christianity and combined with the Pauline notion of "glorious body" or "resurrection body." The "resurrection of the body" is not a grandiose event taking place at the end of times, but rather the already mentioned initiatory "de-coagulation" of the corporeal (endowed-with-form) condition.

A charming Taoist image, describing the one who can undergo any change of state while remaining free and invulnerable, is that of the "flying immortal" (*fei-sien*). Finally, one finds the initiatory and hierarchical distinction between the "earthly immortal" and the "heavenly immortal." This distinction should be attributed to the existence of two types of immunity to changes of state: immunity to the changes proper of the human condition, and immunity to the changes proper of other superior, "heavenly" conditions of being.

*　*　*　*　*

I will not describe here the techniques employed by operative Taoism. Some of these techniques consist of disciplining one's thought; contemplation; yoga-like techniques, based on breathing and on the practice of sex; dietary practices; drugs; forms of practical alchemy; and even a type of physical workout (the so-called *tao-yin*). From an inner perspective, detachment is the main premise, thus, "not to yearn desire," as Lao-tzu himself said, in order to de-coagulate the flux of vital energy. This process is compared to restoring the throne of the One, the legitimate sovereign, who has been deposed by usurpers and by rebellious generals. The technical term "nourishing the spirit" is synonymous of strengthening the One, who sometimes is called the "Great *Yang*." The cold and impersonal magical quality which must be achieved is the opposite of mystical enthusiasm. What is required, instead of moralism, is a balanced neutrality toward both good and evil. This is called "cooling one's heart," or "emptying one's heart." One Taoist text speaks of "the heart, as cold

25

ashes, without emotions or inclinations;" similar expressions are also found in Chuang-tzu. Once this state is achieved, one will perceive the *Tao* and suddenly become aware of being within the Way. Everything else is only a consequence and a consolidation. In Chuang-tzu (VI, 8) seven stages are mentioned in reference to Master Pu-Liang I: 1) he banished from his mind all worldly matters; 2) he banished from his mind all thoughts of men and things; 3) he was able to count his life as foreign to himself; 4) this accomplished, his mind was afterwards clear as the morning; 5) after this he was able to see his own individuality; 6) he was then able to banish all thought of Past and Present; 7) freed from this, he was able to penetrate to the truth that there is no difference between life and death. Once the *Tao* is perceived, the distinction between past and present becomes meaningless. Finally "the mystery unfolds" and a state occurs in which "one is not alive nor dead," to indicate the superiority toward life and death proper to the "transformed" being, who is united to the fixed Principle "from which all mutations derive."

This is the realization which will gradually de-coagulate or "melt" the form, from the subtle to the gross, until the corpse will dissolve (*che-kiai*). In the *Tao-Te-Ching* (ch. 10) there is an explicit reference to this, almost as if to give away a secret teaching, through the initiatory amalgamation of soul and body into the "mysterious Quality." When it comes to written documents, the best available on this subject are gathered in a work of Henri Maspero's ("*Les procedes de nourrir l'esprit vital dans la religione taoste ancienne*," *Journal Asiatique* (219), 1973). Although these techniques are mentioned as early as 400-300 B.C., it is difficult to separate the genuine nucleus of these ideas from what is the product of misunderstandings, misleading interpretations, deviations or degenerations of the doctrine. After all, the Masters explicitly warned that the real key to operative Taoism is not given in writing but is transmitted orally.

Beginning with the Han period, the esoteric Taoism of the "Men of *Tao*" (*tao-che*) became distinct from religious Taoism (*tao-chiao*) and it continued as a secret tradition up to our days. Matgioi (a military man whose Western name was A. de Poupourville), one of the very few Europeans to come in direct contact with the representatives of this tradition, has referred to the existence, among Taoist initiatory groups, of a hierarchy consisting of three degrees. The first degree is that of *tong-sang*, in which a person is initiated to the teachings formulated in the texts. The second degree is that of *phu-tuy*, which includes a deepening of the doctrine, not only on an intellectual level: one must be able to discover the higher and secret meanings contained in the texts by himself, since at this level a major rule would be broken if knowledge was acquired through the help of somebody else. One is admitted to the third and last degree (*phap*) only after undergoing a period of isolation and silence and after this period one is given the full initiation. *Phap* corresponds to the first of the two types of initiate previously described. He is an obscure and powerful being, venerated and ignored, detached from everything and everybody. He is attributed the power of mastering his body and of having full knowledge of the hidden secrets and forces of nature. He corresponds to the figure of the "Immortal" of ancient Taoism (Matjoi, *La voie rationelle*. Paris: 1907, ch. VII).

In Chinese civilization, the other exterior and degenerated forms of religious or semi-shamanic Taoism became discredited and lost ground to the second orthodox teaching, namely Confucianism. Much of Lao-tzu's version of Taoism, also considered as a general conduct of life and as an inner discipline, has been preserved, mixed with Buddhism, in other schools such as Zen (see *Zen: The Religion of the Samurai* by Julius Evola, Holmes Publishing Group, 1994). Zen is still active in Japan and has recently drawn the attention of several Western groups. In Zen, the elimination of the Ego and its tensions ("emptiness") and anti-intellectualism constitute a path leading to a higher spontaneity and perfection, which are not confined to an ascetical or mystical world, but which are rather applied to all aspects of life. In Zen, an enlightenment, usually conceived as a sudden and abrupt change of level, induces a change of polarity, and brings the Ego back to its true center by uniting it with the Great Principle.

NOTES

[1] *The Texts of Taoism*. Translated by James Legge. (New York: Dover Publications, 1962), Ch. 38.
[2] Ibid., *Tao-Te-Ching*, ch.5.
[3] *Chuang-tzu*, XII, 3.
[4] Ibid., *Tao-Te-Ching*, ch. 25.
[5] Ibid., *Chuang-tzu*, XX, 7.
[6] *Chung Yung*. Translated by Ezra Pound. (NY: New Directions, 1951), XXVI, 6.
[7] Ibid., I, 1.
[8] *Texts of Taoism, Chuang-tzu*, V, 5.
[9] Henri Maspero, (*Le Taoisme*: Paris, 1950), 40.